T5-DHH-551

DEAR FUTURE
BOYFRIEND

AIDAN --
CAN YOU BELIEVE
THESE DIDN'T WORK?

DARTMOUTH

OCT '09

DEAR FUTURE BOYFRIEND

BOYFRIEND

Cristin O'Keefe Aptowicz

WORDSMITH PRESS

Copyright 2007 by Cristin O'Keefe-Aptowicz
ISBN 978-1-893972-27-8 by

The Wordsmith Press
11462 East lane
Whitmore Lake, MI 48189

810-231-5435
www.thewordsmithpress.com
info@thewordsmithpress.com

All rights reserved under international and pan-American copyright conventions. Published in the United States by The Wordsmith Press, Whitmore Lake, MI. No part of this book may be reproduced or transmitted in any form or by any means, electronic or mechanical, including photocopying and recording, without written permission from the publisher.

Cover design by Claudia Sherman. claudelemeonde@gmail.com

PREFACE TO THIS EDITION

The first edition of *Dear Future Boyfriend* was written, printed and pasted together in the computer lab basement of an NYU dorm.

At the time, I remember thinking: "I don't know how I will ever write a better book."

Such is the unstoppable hubris of the 20-year-old poet.

The original little blue book went from being a backpack staple for all my early performances, to finding its way onto merch tables at festivals and national poetry slams, to eventually snuggling up next zines and chapbooks at independent and online bookstores across the country.

Almost a decade later, it's been surreal and humbling creating the expanded edition you are holding in your hands now. I spent weeks combing through old journals, lit mags and sentimental boxes of letters to find previously unpublished poetry from ages 16 to 21 to use for this volume. The experience was not unlike taking a beautiful earnest cheese grater—one with unforgivably poor grammar skills— and rubbing it all over my sterling silver ego and previously proud heart.

I'll be honest and say that I never understood why boys didn't like me back... until I read my old high school and college poetry. Then the answer became so apparent, in all its rambling stalker-like glory.

But how many of us can read the poetry we wrote as teen-agers without wanting to ignite the whole mess on fire, followed quickly by igniting ourselves?

And yet once this burning embarrassment subsided, I began to actually read the work. It was not perfect, clearly, but I soon grew to admire my younger self's lack of self-con-sciousness. I became charmed by the awkward attempts at love poetry and the "me-thinks-you-protest-too-much" platitudes about being over heartbreak. I laughed out loud at my shameless goofiness.

I realized that in the years since the original *Dear Future Boyfriend* was published, the role poetry played in my life had evolved without me even realizing it. The more you write, I feel, the more you begin to use poetry as a filter. When something strange happens in your life and the ex-perience rattles around your ribs or skull for too long, you start writing a poem about it, and in doing so, you hope to sift out the meaning of the experience.

But when you are first starting out, the poetry *is* the experience.

You don't write a poem about how you wish a guy was in love with you; You write a poem to *make* that guy fall in love with you.

The work from that early era of mine was just that direct. It didn't want to change the world – it was already convinced that it could! The poems were honest and sweet and delusional and stubborn, but ultimately unapologetic. I began to understand what attracted readers to this book was not that I was such a unique and exceptional young writer; it was that it was written

by an unabashedly and utterly normal young writer.
So with that, I welcome you to this expanded volume – my own private time capsule!

I hope that you'll enjoy all the scrappy sincerity I feel it exudes as it tells the story of a young poet trying to find her voice and a young woman trying to find her footing in this riotously unfair yet beautiful world.

Cristin O'Keefe Aptowicz
December 2006

p.s. – In the original first edition of *Dear Future Boyfriend*, my "introduction" was a lengthy transcribed rant decrying my ability to write. It was left anonymously on the Poemfone* voicemail during the month which I was the chosen poet. I've opted to include to this introduction in this edition as well. I do so not only because the rant is utterly hilarious and horrifying in its knife-to-the-gut, worst-nightmare version of what someone could spontaneously say about your writing, but because I really marvel at my initial moxie in choosing to include it. In showcasing the worst criticism I'd yet received at the top of my book, I was telling the world I knew the ego-crushing revulsion that could greet these poems upon the release of the book... but I just didn't care. I wanted to get my words out there. That alone might make it the most poetic thing in the whole book.

* - Poemfone was a NYC-based arts project which chose a different poet each month to leave a poem a day for people to dial in and listen.

DEAR FUTURE BOYFRIEND

BOYFRIEND

(this is what I sound like)

poems by

Cristin O'Keefe Aptowicz

by the Guy Who Hated My Stuff on Poemfone
(dictated directly off the Poemfone voicemail
but without permission, so shhh....)

With patience, I have heard your poetry like every single other crap that I have heard on the poem phone for as far back as I can remember when Penny Cade? Penny Arcade? Come on in 95 and 96?

I really don't understand what it is you people call poetry. I mean, I honestly don't *understand* what it is that you call poetry, this crap... I mean, do you? Are honestly *proud* of what you write? Do honestly sit down, aware of what you are doing, *and with full comprehension of what it is that you are doing*, say to people, let alone strangers, that this is what you write?

If it's friends, maybe, out of pity they might say: *Yes, your work is alright*. But a stranger? I mean it's just nonsense. I honestly don't know what it is you people do with your lives, what it is you really do, what your profession is, but I hope, *god*, I hope you don't expect, in any way shape or form to be *remembered* for what it is your write.

I don't say this as hard person putting down another person, because if I wrote something and it was shit, I would expect people to tell me it was garbage, that way I could improve, I could understand what it was that I was lacking. And not from one person, as many people as I could possibly get an opinion to see if my work is at all worthwhile reading.

But your stuff is crap, genuine gar-*bage*.

And this might just be me, I mean, maybe I am the only one who views your stuff as crap. Maybe I'm only that calls once in a while with curiosity to see if anything has improved in this poemfone. I man, maybe it's just me.

So it's just one person, but your stuff is crap.

TABLE OF CONTENTS

MOTHER

When I told my mother
I wanted to be a veterinarian
when I grew up,

she told me
that vets kill puppies and kittens
and stuck needles into horses
and bunnies with cancer.

When I told my mother
I wanted to be zoo-keeper
when I grew up,

she told me
that animals in captivity
are still wild animals, and hence
could attack even the friendliest
of caretakers, usually tearing them
to shreds and eating the remains.

You see, my mom and I
had a lot of time to talk
about these things: I was the last
of the Aptowicz brood.

Always too young and too small
to go on the backpacking trips
and nature hikes that formed
my brother and sister: the scientists.

No, it was always just mom and me,

a stack of books and NPR coming through
the radio like the voice of God.

Mom never liked my career choices much,
but I knew I was on the right track
when one day over a bowl of alphabet soup
I asked her:

Hey mom,
how come there are such things
as bad words?

And she said:

Honey, there is no such thing
as a "bad word." Only words
that aren't appropriate
for all situations.
For instance,
you should never say
the word "shit"
in front of a nun.

You see, she gave me that,
she gave me the gift of words,
she gave me the power of words,
and I never considered it a privilege.

But my mom grew up in a time
when words were being redefined.
Words like gender, power, class
and revolution.

She grew up in a house
where a wrench spray-painted gold
would serve as a shower dial,
and a father overseas would somehow
support a wife and four kids
left stateside, being my mother,
her sister and two sons, who wouldn't
even recognize their father
when he returned home
four years later.

Eating meat once a week,
recycling shoes to the next kid in line,
and using babysitting money
to buy groceries,

even my mom knew the score.

So although she was top of her class,
editor of the school literary magazine,
editor of the school newspaper,
the National Merit Scholar with
the three newspaper a day habit,
she still had to hear them tell her:

The scholarship
is not going to be for English.
If you want to go to college at all,
it will have to be for science.

So my mother, the biologist,
met my father, the chemical engineer,
and together they produced three beautiful kids,
one of which my mom would make sure
wouldn't feel the burn she was forced to feel.

One government paycheck and three kids
under the age of four doesn't go very far,
but mom always made sure we had books,
ever if it meant we rolled pennies
instead of dice, or bought our Christmas
gifts from our neighbor's garage sale.

People always ask me
why I make such a big deal
correcting them saying:

No, it is not
Cristin Aptowicz.

It's Cristin O'Keefe Aptowicz.

It's just one word, they say,
it shouldn't make that much difference.

But I know the differences words make.
It is a gift my mother gave me.

And I honor her
every time I put pen to paper,
every time I put word to lip,
and every time I sign my name

because I know that in order
for me, Cristin O'Keefe Aptowicz,
to be who I am, to live how I live,
to write how I write,

it took
Maureen Anne O'Keefe,
the visionary, the writer,

to become
Maureen Aptowicz,
the wife, the mother.

My mother said
she'd never trade
any of us kids in for a novel
or a job at the New York Times,
though the way we behave sometimes
she says she'd consider it.

But I know she's only joking
because I have never seen her
look so proud, or smile so bright,
as when I finally told her
what I wanted to do,
and she said:

You know what, honey?

I think
Cristin O'Keefe Aptowicz
is the perfect name

for a writer.

CHECKLIST

People who think you should date me:
Your mother, check.
Your two little sisters, check.
All three of your brothers, check.
Your dad, "Invite her for dinner!" check.
Your friends, except for that lame-ass,
money-obsessed misogynist, check.
You, the jury is still out,
but I think your subconscious is a check.
Me, check.
My friends,
except for the one that dated you, check.
Fate, check.
Modern science, check.
God, if you believed in one, check.

SHORT LIST

If I were to name all the men I've ever kissed
it would not even fill up a post-it note,
even if you wrote in fancy, cursive script,
even if you allowed me to count 11-year-olds
as men, even if you counted closed-mouth kissing,
even if the post-it note was not a post-it note for humans,
but a post-it note created for ants that could only be
used by ants wearing business suits and spectacles,
who spent their afternoons doodling
on these post-it notes while buying and selling
stock on abandoned Doritos and that mint
I spit out onto the grass that last time
I kissed you.

BROKENDOWNMACHINE

1.
INBREEDING
I am very much against inbreeding,
except when you say that
you love me like a sister.

2.
THE PLAN
I'll just keep being
really smart and pretty
until you realize it
and fall in love with me.

3.
OVERCOMPENSATING
This is what I feel people are doing
while I see them pawing each other
in public.

They are just overcompensating,
I think, for the fact that they can't
have me.

4.
OPTIMIST
Steven,
the guy who gave me my AIDS test,
was really cute.

5.
I AM SMARTER THAN HER
and that is my only consolation.

EQUINOX

Night was distancing itself
caged in starlight and missing satellites
it was too afraid of us quicksilver teenagers
with change in our pockets
so you and I found refuge
under a buzzing electric sky

You called me Persephone
and said I had just paid for
the last seed eaten
so we could be above ground
unrestrained and laughing

Winter birthed spring
and died in the process
we did not see her go but
we could feel under
unnatural sidewalks
crocus buds swimming upward
we smiled at spring
as she tripped toward us,
fingers in her mouth

(and yes, the streetlamps spat
an uneasy moonlight
we were crooked fisted
swinging in an unexpected warmth
our grins clinking
we knew the pregnancy of time)

I remember we were lying in the street
red-faced and trembling
when you touched me

NIGHTFALL

I was bearing down on the night
swinging from a maple tree
five miles from the city limits

you were lying on the hood of your jeep
sucking the moon's vapors
trying to fasten your day
onto something cool and dark
your eyes exposed like comets

and the radio was turned down low
playing some jazz song that
coated the grass in magic
sweeping leaves into dance
shaking air from the clouds

I can see the city from here,
I told you, and you didn't believe me
so I pointed it out to you
when you reached the top

we sat there for a long time
watching the city lights
filter through clouds touching
each other's arms
and hands searching
the wind for incoming stars
we were seamless and opened

and we should have stayed there
all night sipping the sky through our eyes

kissing each others fingertips until
we shone like the sun

instead we climbed down,
earthbound meteors, tired and dirty,
navigating past cicada shells

we drove home and
the stars hid behind streetlamps
the moon seared quietly
its song no match for the city

TRANSIENT

The night air feels unused
swimming up from asphalt
curling rings around my legs

I think back to February
and old winter winds,
of us at the station,
our knees kinked up to our ears
speaking in tongues
avoiding eye contact

I box myself at midnight
crossing the railroad tracks
a block away from your house

I press against a tree
trying to leak these thoughts of you
they stay unmoved, indifferent
your house denies asylum

the bark is discordant
against my skin creating
imprints, maps on legs
and arms leading nowhere
lines that spell nothing

I fasten my intentions
to your kitchen window
the lights are
silent breathing endless

I stand at the boundaries
of your yard wondering
where the neutrality ends
and you begin

NIGHT VISION OF A WOMAN GONE

Momma Downs' hands were clean & strong
her hips wide from housing life

every morning she tied her hair up in a braid
the color of urban moonlight

Momma Downs smelled of children of warmth
and fresh scrubbed skin

I would watch her as she walked in the kitchen
her skirt dancing above the floor boards

Momma Downs laughed like cool water
falling over sharp stone

her wrists were translucent she seemed invincible
eyes feral as the wind

Momma Downs left tins cans for me in her driveway
an invitation to visit,

from the porch I could see her over the stove
she was a woman who spilled

humanity into shells of disbelief and
she was making eggs

Happy Birthday Haiku

I took the subway
one stop too far writing a
poem about you.

HAIKU ABOUT LOVE AND POP CULTURE

In a frictionless world
the mystery machine would
go on forever.

When two strands of life
smash into one another and become one,
that is called fusion; cold fusion is a myth
In order for two things to become one
you need heat, a lot of it.

And there's always been a lot of heat
between us, Jason, whenever you get pedantic
and ramble on about science:

All your swan's neck flasks and balding
Madame Curies, all your anecdotes
about Dick Feynman's van with his own
Nobel Prize-winning Feynman's Diagrams
on the side and when people used to honk
their horns, roll down their windows
and yell:

    Hey! Do you realize those are
    Feynman's Diagrams
    on the side of your van?

Dick would just answer back:

    Yes, I am Richard Feynman!

God, I adore scientists, or maybe just you,
Jason, because you will never love me
as much as you love process
    that research, hypo,
    experiment, record,

        experiment, record,
        experiment, record,
        conclusion, thesis,
        satisfaction and contempt
that is bred into you at every lab hour,
every No-Doze stoned study group,
every opportunity to dig up dinosaur bones
in Nova Scotia so that you can send me
a postcard covered in dust.

I wrote a poem about you last week
swearing up and down that I would write
        no more about you,
        no more about you,
        no more about you
but this is not about you, Jason!
This is about science!
Your life choice! Your dream world!
And I have to write about you, Jason,
because you are my science,
because science is your god

And no, you do not dictate what I do
or say, and no, you did not create me,
but you do control my temperatures
you do influence my tides,
making me rise and fall and rise
        and fall and rise and fall
        and rise
according to how you see the moon

I've had enough poets, Jason

And I know that you get shy because
you think you don't have any metaphors,
just that old Bunsen burner
you fished out of the trash.
You called it a relic and wrote your name
on it, saying you wanted to attach yourself
to a 'pre-er' science, a time when less was known.

You are beautiful in ways you aren't even aware of.

And I'm trying to explain this all to you
over breakfast, but there is a science to loving
someone, and I have failed that course
every time I signed up for it.

I just keep thinking about the Heisenberg
Uncertainty Principle which states,
no matter what, there will always be
something compelling our non-love,
our non-togetherness so I'll just keep quiet
and eat my florentine omelet, if you please.

And you can talk some more about
you favorite story, 'Spontaneous Generation!'
the concept that mice came from wheat,
and flies from wheat, and smart little Louie Pasteur
proved them all wrong, and purified milk as well

Nothing comes from nothing! you say

And I want to catalogue our experiences
in a white lab coat with goggles,
I want to offer up my love on a Petri dish

asking you to stain my culture
and watch it grow

Because you are my science, Jason,
you are my endless hypothesis,
and I am tired of the
    experiment, record,
    experiment, record
Get me to my conclusion, Jason!
Prove my thesis statement,
that states that
    you squared
    plus me squared
    equals
    love squared

And if you think this is a joke, Jason,
why don't you adapt your science
and prove me wrong.

LOVE POEM

I took a deep breath,
and told the audience
that you were in the theatre,
made a gesture, and their heads
shifted and craned to look at you.
They smiled.

Then I took another deep breath,
stepped back and closed my eyes.
I had told the cast of the play
I was opening for, that this was
my kamikaze night: crash and burn.
I was all alone on that stage and
you were all alone in the audience.

Afterwards,
we went to dinner
at the only restaurant in New York
that you like, Chat 'n' Chew,
and I got us free dessert by singing
Happy Birthday so loudly, that
the entire restaurant was clapping
their hands by the end, and I didn't
even know the guy.

She's so special, the waitresses
told you when they crowded around
our table. One gave you a little
push on the back of your shoulder.
Do you realize that, she asked.
Yes, you said. Do you, she asked.
When they left, I smiled

at you over my coffee mug.
Magic, I said.
I said I was magic.

Later that night,
you fell asleep hours before me,
lying in my roommates bed.
I was flat on my back, staring
at the ceiling, trying not
to think about that poem.

Sometimes words are really just words.

LAST NIGHT

My friend Amanda is house-sitting
at this really swank apartment
and she has invited all of her friends
to sleep over.

Everybody is fucking in new beds tonight,
except me.

I'm reading a *National Geographic*
from 1994.

The plight of the panda
was never so sad.

SOMERTON STATION

is the train station
near my house

where nothing
romantic
ever happened
to me.

Mostly just
sad things.

Mostly just
things that never
worked out.

Because nothing
ever works out
for me.

Because nobody
loves me and
I love nobody.

Writing this poem
is making me
sad.

ODE TO THE PERSON
WHO STOLE MY FAMILY'S LAWN GNOME
for Kev

Are you sinister?

Because I think you're sinister.

Are you evil?

Because I think you're evil.

You wait until my family is out watching fireworks
on the Fourth of July and you up and steal
my family's lawn gnome.

Did you want to register a reaction with us?

Was that your intent?

Did you watch us as we stumbled around in the dark,
wishing, hoping, praying, "Well, maybe the wind
just blew him to some other part of the lawn," but he
was not to be found that night, or the next morning.

He has a name—
A name my brother gave him
when we were all younger.

Did you know that?

When you pedaled furiously away,
did you whisper into his pointy elfin ears,
"Hutchison Farf, now you are mine?"

Why do you need a lawn gnome?

Why do *you* need a lawn gnome?

I can tell you why we needed one.
It was used to cure my brother of his fear
of little people after he saw *The Wizard of Oz*
and began having nightmares of being trampled
by tiny feet. My mother purchased him from
a flea market in Lancaster and told my brother
that they could be friends. My brother was not
assured. He did not like the idea of a person much
much older who was the same size
as his five year old self.

But it worked.

And Hutchison Farf has had his place in our yard
for over seven years now.

Well, until you stole him, thief.

Until you kidnapped him, scoundrel.

Until you took him away and did god knows what to him,
you tiny-cocked jerk!

Why do you need a lawn gnome?

Was it for decoration?

Did you not notice that brand-spanking new
"Fat Woman Bending Over" cut-out two doors down?
Or how about the perilously perched kitten clinging
to the Gantert's garage? Or what about the over-sized,
iridescent snail inexplicably slurping across the
Muldoon's lawn just twenty feet away tops?

Why a lawn gnome?

Are you fucked up in the head?

Do you have absolutely no taste in lawn accouterments?

It's a fucking cement gnome!
What was the attraction? I am very fucking curious!

My mother said I should calm down.

Maybe even
forgive you.

That you were probably some prankster
8-year-old,
you rat bastard motherfucker.

But I can't forget.

I've grown suspicious of my neighborhood watch.

I've grown envious of my neighbor's untouched cow
placards, that read "Crowther's: 823 Herschel Road."

So I've counted the inventory.

Missing: One, Hutchison Farf
Height: 12 inches, including permanently stuck-
              on cement cap with cement bell
Eyes: Blue
Hair: Red
Beard: Red
Last seen: Frozen in Jig Position, upper center part of
              my lawn, slightly obscured by shrubbery
Owner's Heart: Broken

I tried to lodge a complaint
but the police just laughed.

THE WORST VALENTINES GIFT I EVER GOT

We had been dating for three months
and he got me a mug which read:
Friends are people who never let you
forget all the stupid things you've done.

THE WORST ANNIVERSARY GIFT I EVER GOT

A 25% off coupon
for a discount bra store
at the largest outlet mall
in Pennsylvania

PROMS

I went to 8 proms in high school.

Although I would later change my mind
I never liked my dates enough to live
out any of the stereotypes:
kissing during the last song,
the hotel room afterwards,
perhaps the loosening of virginities,
if not the loss of them all together,
being in love forever.

I keep all the corsages in my closet,
drying still on the hooks on the door.
Some nights I try one on,
some nights, two, some, three,
and some lonely long summer nights
I try on all eight, and imagine all the dates
converging into my bedroom,
thinking me beautiful in pjs and flowers.

DEATH FARM

Everyone knew Andy's brother, Mike,
worked at the Death Farm, thought no one knew
exactly what he did. All anybody could really say,
was that
Mike left at 6 in the morning and
returned 12 hours later,
looking pretty much the same.

Andy thought I deserved to know this
about his brother, Mike, considering that
I was visiting for the weekend from Philadelphia,
and he wanted to assure me that Mike was a good guy,
and that he would never harm anyone,
and that a job's a job.
When I told him I didn't know what Death Farm was
Andy nearly drove off the road.

Every city and every town has its stories.
In my neighborhood in Philadelphia, we'd stay up late
and go to some shit-filled pond where some kid
was supposed
to have drowned years ago and
they never found the body
and we'd scare ourselves hoarse screaming that we could
see him under the water, see his hands reaching up at us.

This is how a lot of us got out first kisses,
screaming and reaching towards the one person
we wanted to make us feel safe.

In Paolo, in Central Pennsylvania, where's Andy's from,
there was the Death Farm, which wasn't so much a ghost story
and certainly not romantic.

The story goes, Andy told me, that sometime
in the 60s or the 70s,the US government bought up
the Trainer family's huge orchard
and let the place go wild.

Then, they built the facility deep in the land
so no one could see
and kept it all hush hush what they were doing.

But somehow it got out,
that the 136-acres of what used to be an orchard
were now littered with bodies,
bodies that were donated to science,
bodies that the FBI would then cut, stab, shoot, submerge
under water for days, carve letters into, hand with ropes,
run over with cars and do whatever else the crazy people
of the world would do to another human being
at the time, and then the bodies
would be placed all over what used to be orchard.

Then trainees or FBI investigators would go out and find them,
study the effects had on the bodies,
create theories about the mind
of the killer, try to understand what happened and why.
The first time I heard about it,
I thought Andy was shitting me.
He offered to drive by it, but I wouldn't let him,

Eventually we did, late at night on Sunday,

and the place was packed, irresistible to teenagers.
Everyone got out of their cars,
and walked along side the high,
electric fence, putting face to metal
and peering into the brush,
claiming to see a hand or a boot sticking out
of drainage pipe
or floating in the shallow creek. But no one could actually
prove a thing. It was kind of funny in a sick way.

People kept asking Andy about what his brother did,
first to get his goat, but then out of sincere curiosity,
and he answered them, the way he answered me
with the truth.

Mike never told anyone what he did.

He wasn't allowed.

I didn't get to meet Mike, until Sunday,
when Andy got sick and Andy's mom got
Mike to drive me the hour's drive
to the train station.

We kept quiet for the most of the ride.
The radio was broke, so Mike had a boombox,
and we listened to a mix tape he made
heavy metal and hard rock, mostly:
I love rock n roll, put another
dime in the jukebox, baby.

But night was closing in, the hour's drive
seemed to be taking three times that amount.
It would be a lie to say I didn't feel scared,

that I didn't want to jump out of the car,
although I really knew nothing about Andy's brother.

It would be a lie to say that I didn't suddenly believe
what I had been hearing from all of Andy's friends,
that Mike was the guy in charge of screwing around
with the bodies, and this is how he got his rocks off.
I mean, I knew it was bullshit, but I couldn't say
at age 16, all alone in that car, that I wasn't scared.
The radio was broke. The street was so dark.

Then, after about 45 minutes into the trip, Mike spoke.
You know, I read this real interesting thing yesterday,
he began, clearing his throat, *I read that babies*
remember what it's like to be in the womb
up until the age of 2 or 3. That if you ask them
what it's like, they say, something like, you know,
it was warm, and it was really dark and wet.
Isn't that amazing, he said.

Yeah, I replied.

We smiled at each other. Simple.
He let me out at the train station and I thanked him.

I never talked to Mike again, and never went back
to Paolo and the last time I really talked to Andy
was when he took my cubby friend in Philly
to her senior prom.

But last spring, I was at Bard, and I bumped into him.
I asked him about his life, and Paolo. He said that

the Death Farm is still open,
but that Mike has quit.

He works at Hershey now, he said,
he's in charge of the kisses.

PETAH HAIKU

like the crisp white moon
reflecting the light of the
sun, am I to you.

SEÑOR YOGURT
"I'm not just a snack;
I'm a low fat sour cream substitute!"

Señor Yogurt was the imaginary character
we made up as metaphor for your machismo.

He lived in a mouse hole in your bathroom
and would scold you for your sloppiness.

He would write poetry for you to use,
but you wouldn't.

He told you to shower more,
but instead you'd just sleep.

He told you how to style your hair,
all the good pick-up lines and loved

to point out all the basic opportunities
he thought you were letting slip

through your fingers. Even now, I can't
explain why we thought it was so funny,

but we really did. When it finally
hatched out that you and I liked each other

but some how ruined it, we soon forgot
about Señor Yogurt. Neither of us wanted

to hear his opinions on the matter. Now
when I tell people about Señor Yogurt,

they roll their eyes. No one cares
about Señor Yogurt. They only care

about the terrible coming apart.
That's the story.

Well, Señor Yogurt,
this poem is for you.

SIDE EFFECTS

My friend's mother is a doctor, and she says
that people like medication that has side effects
better than ones that don't because it's proof
that the medicine is doing something.
An old boyfriend once told me
that he masturbated to me so much
he accidentally water-proofed his hand.
Whenever you write me a letter,
I treat myself to ice cream.

SIGN

I like my coffee
with 2 sugars and 2 creams,
unless I'm in a diner
then 3 sugars and 2 half-and-halfs,
unless I'm a café
then it's a half-mocha, half-espresso
concoction or dark French-pressed.

And yet, when we went out,
you ordered me a tea,

with a big soggy lemon, no less.

MY PARENTS

are in love and don't try
to tell them otherwise or
they will get really angry.

Subway

I have yet to write
a happy poem
on the subway.

Except for the one
I wrote when I discovered
that you were in love
with me.

But then, it turned out
that you were, in fact,
in love with
someone
else.

So now
that poem
is not so happy
anymore.

Ex-Boyfriend

When I went to the WaWa
to see if my ex-boyfriend still worked there,
I discovered it has been turned
into a funeral home.

Now how am I supposed to kill him?

I think it takes me longer than most
to get over my ex-boyfriends.
Or rather, ex-boy*friend*,
for there is only one
only one who counts.

The one, the He,
who dumped me
for that trampy, white-trash,
I-want-to-get-with-you-at-a-dairy-queen,
ill-mannered, submissive, giggling,
tight-jeaned, loose-kneed,
pornette patriarch poster girl
Marissa.

Marissa, whom he met
at a bowling alley.

My friends tell me
that I need to stop harping
on him, and just move on.

Fuck you.

See, I have some sort of emotional problem
that prevents me from getting in touch
with my anger, except for one situation,
the one, the he, the ex-boyfriend.

I worship my ex-boyfriend
like a bad star.

I cannot tell you his name
because I cannot be positive
that you are not his friend
the he has sent to spy on me
because he is secretly in love
with me but afraid that I'll find out .

If you are my ex-boyfriend,
then you are reading this by accident.

It you are my ex-boyfriend,
then inside your chest
beats a heart made of
deformed Beanie Animals.

Symbolism.

I never loved you.
I keep you hair in envelopes in my closet.
I am the one who has your Klimt book.

Only one of these things is true.

EX-BOYFRIEND!!!

When will you die
so that I can start writing
good ex-boyfriend poetry
dead ex-boyfriend poetry
without the requisite
live ex-boyfriend bitterness.

The last time I went on a date
with someone new, I chewed
all the leather off my sleeves
waiting for him to choose
a song at the jukebox.

I am not made
to date someone new.

EX-BOYFRIEND!!

Your cologne is everywhere.

EX-BOYFRIEND!!

I have a mug with your name on it!

EX-BOYFRIEND!!

I want to kill you with gasoline
and cheesecake!

I want to kill you with gasoline
and comic books!

I want to kill you with gasoline
and prom pictures!

EX-BOYFRIEND!!

How long do I have to lay on this floor
before you fall in love with me again?

PLACES I HAVE NEVER BEEN KISSED

bookstores, beaches, carnivals, funerals,
basements, weddings, family reunions,
my boyfriend's bedroom, my parent's bedroom,
malls, mcdonalds, a new york city park,
in a pond, in a pool, in a prom dress,
nevada.

Hard Bargain

I am auctioning off my virginity
to the highest bidder.

I am not, and let me make
this perfectly clear, I am not
being metaphorical here.

I want cold hard cash
for my tight hot ethics.

I am sick of my virginity.

Back in the day, when we were eight, shit,
everyone was saving themselves for marriage,
or at least college, or at least a stable relationship
but now I've got friends' little sisters giving
me advice on handjobs,

And I don't have to put up with this crap
because I'm in college and if there is one thing
I've learned about virginity in college
is that it is, at best, an anecdote,
and not having a good anecdote is one thing,
but the reactions are a whole other story.

All the girls with their:
Well, don't worry.
You're bound to find someone.

And all the guys with their,
and sometimes these are guys
that I am interested in,

all the guys with their:

>Oh.
>Well, that explains a lot.

I don't need to be putting up with this shit.

I am turning 20 in 149 days, and if there was
one thing that I have learned about virginity
anecdotes, is that when you turn 20, the stories
go from charming and poignant
to depressing and pathetic.

So that's when it came to me:

Prostitution

What a great foray into the sexual experience
and let's be honest, what a great anecdote.

My plan, at first, was sell everything that I have
of merit, buy a round trip ticket to San Francisco,
rent a car and even though I don't drive,
drive that car
down the darkest, poorest, scariest alley
in all of San Fran,
the one that I read about
in those Covenant House pamphlets
my mom would get from the Jehovah's Witnesses,
and I would find the youngest, most heroin-addicted,
wild-eyed, freshfaced prostitute and open up
my car door and flash 200 crisp one dollar bills
and say

>Get in.

And I wouldn't tell him I'm a virgin.
I would tell him I'm a nympho, and I would take
him to a fancy hotel, and clean him up,
and lay him down on silk sheets, and fuck him
like I've never fucked before, because I haven't
ever fucked before.

But then, just as this fantasy gets good, I remember:
syphilis, gonorrhea, hepatitis A, B, C, the clap,
body lice, genital warts, crabs, scabies, Chlamydia,
and AIDS.

And then it hit me

Sell... *myself?*

Fucking brilliant.

Fuck, I would be this thing,
this whole underground sex world thing.
Business men from Tokyo would be calling
Business men in Wall Street, who would be
calling up Heidi Fleiss in prison asking:
How do I get a piece of that?

Rich kids from LA would be logging in to
www.hymen.com for hourly updates.

Entire Italian villages would pool their money
so that I could lose it with the town schlong:
Ernesto, with the enormous cock that smells
suspiciously like flan and is crooked to the left.

I could get corporate sponsors:

This defloweration is brought to you
by Ivory Soap, 99.44% pure!

I could sell the rights to HBO.

I would have to shave my pubic hair
into the Nike Swoosh logo.

And after it was all over. And the hype dies
down, I'll sit in my new 36th floor apartment,
on my sofa made of twenties, and I'll make
myself some tea, and pull down the curtains,
and turn off the lights, and close my eyes,
and lie in the dark of room,
and try to remember
what it was like
to be

a virgin

but until then,
let the bidding begin.

WHAT I WAS THINKING WHEN WE WERE DRIVING AROUND AND YOU DIDN'T THINK TO ASK ME WHAT I WAS THINKING

If you don't turn off
the goddamn Garth Brooks music
and turn around and look at me
I'm going to punch a hole
in your fucking throat.

Satie's *Gymonopedie*

used to remind me of you,
until I listened to it too much,
and now it reminds me
of not being with you.

The same thing happened
with Beck's *Girl of my Dreams*,
Springstein's *Ballad of Tom Joad*,
and Nick Drake's *Black Eyed Dog*.

Music has proved an unstable substitute
and just as well.

END

I have written too often
of your lips, their indifferent flatness,
the pressure they yield on words,

but I have forgotten
almost every thing else,
your speech, the texture
of the palms of your hands.

I have battled time for you
but there have been too many
causalities: most recently
hope, followed by nostalgia.

So wave the white flag, tired,
I have lost all purpose and direction
I have grown sick of trembling.

I throw you and watch you sink,
slow, slow, slow until
you are nothing.

You didn't fight it
or at least,
I didn't notice.

For Phil on the Occasion of His 21st Birthday

Summertime, and we couldn't raise our voices
high enough. 21, and you breathed warm air
You with your wine-colored cheeks
I could do nothing but blush

High enough? 21, and you breathed warm air
and all I could do was taste the sweat of your words
I could do nothing but blush
Lauren and Erin were slick with kisses

And all I could do was taste the sweat of your words
I arched my body forward and we laughed, breathed
Lauren and Erin were slick with kisses
21, and you were the most beautiful creature I'd seen

I arched my body forward and we laughed, breathed
All I wanted to do was write poetry about this:
21, and you were the most beautiful creature I'd seen
We sunk into each other's skin on the couch

All I wanted to do was write poetry about this
night: you and me and the world, dancing
we sunk into each other's skin. On the couch
I could have laughed all

night: you and me and the world, dancing,
we swing our bodies until they were one
I could have laughed all
summer: it was almost over

We swung our bodies until they were one
Tired, we leaned into each other to get home
Summer: it was almost over
If I could take any of this back

Tired, we leaned into each other to get home
Summertime and we couldn't raise our voices
If I could take any of this back
You and your wine-colored cheeks.

Why I Avoid Eye Contact

You make me happy
and you are not
a responsible enough
person to hold that
kind of position
in my life.

Last night, the couple next door were at it again. He spoke German like a man off a language cassette and she giggled sweetly, loudly. Lovemaking sounds so different here, like time doesn't exist, like this isn't a cheap hotel, like I am not listening, crouched tight in my bed. Kim says we got the rooms cheap because the owner thinks we are lesbians. He speaks a soft and beautiful English. His cheeks are red; Good Year, Happy Year, he said greeting us with our keys as we stumbled in late New Years.

We were tired and beaten. Festivals on the Champs-Elsyée left us dodging bottle rockets and the plump wet meat of lips. *Bonne Année*, they would slur wrapping their fingers around our thighs and necks. We could even see the metro. Later we sat in our quiet room, slumped over butter cookies and juice that we lifted from a marché in Pigalle. Maybe it's a custom, Kim said, shrugging off the images of the night: the strange optimism, the ecstasy, the promise of new things, the sick flattery of hands, the strain of eyes.

The couple next door moved in two days later. Kim says the man looks cruel (she saw him on the way to the toilette) and I worry when the sex becomes too hard, when the grunts become overly male and the armoir bangs anxiously against the wall that separates us. Kim hears nothing of this. She sleeps well and deep. She only knows the quick Swedes next door who flick up the stairs with tiny leather framed legs then spend the afternoon smoking up and listening to the Stones and the Doors.

Our hotel is tiny and the windows open up to an apartment complex. On New Year's, we hung out them and
wished *Bonne Année* to the lingering French who smoke
on their balconies. They raised their wine bottles, un-
fazed. I wonder if they know we look into their windows,
Kim and I both in the afternoon and me, alone, into the
night. I wonder if they realized what I have seen: all the
early morning lovemaking on counters, the nights spent
alone in kitchen, the angry telephone whirled in the air.
They don't appear to, they lift their bottles fearlessly,
Bonne Année.

Kim is asleep now. We went to Versailles in the morning
and we wilted like flowers when it rained. Our hotel
room is warm (and quiet, the Germans and Swedes are
loose on the city). We joked about the concierge, his limp
smile and soft voice and then she slipped between the
covers while I kept watch. She says it is forbidden for me
to sleep during the day: *Interdit!* She says it will keep me
up nights and it's true.

Kim falls asleep so quickly. I sit in a stiff backed chair
eating what's left of the bread we brought for tomorrow's
breakfast. I watch Kim, all damp curl and open mouth. I
understand why the concierge thinks we are lovers: she is
very beautiful. Outside, the Paris rain has stopped and the
sky is clear. It's time for dinner but I'll let Kim sleep.

If someone asked me, I would say the Germans are at
Sacre-Coeur, the Sacred Heart, trying to find ecstasy
between the old stone walls and the cityscape that took
centuries to build. I would say that the Swedes are at Pere
Lachaise; the male Swede says that they visit Jim's grave
everyday. I picture them tomb-side, thankful that the rain

has ended so that they can do another etching before the guard stops them: *James Douglas Morrison* and a date they can never get right.

And I would say I would be here, rubbing tired eyes and cursing my body for its maladjustment, slouching forehead against window. And that Kim would be here, too, asleep and that Paris would be where it is: behind my window and over the balcony, pressed into the streets like a scrapbook, the Seine sleeping soundly in its own bed.

We would all sigh deeply.

The rain has stopped and there is so little to do.

RUN FOR THE BORDER
A Pantoum for Bob, Issac, Craig
and the rest of the Roosevelt Mall Skateboarding Crew

Ah, shit, man, are you kidding me?
No, no, no, ah, shit, man, you're kidding me!
Skater guys dig Taco Bell!
I've been in the mood for nachos.

No, no, no, ah, shit, man, you're kidding me!
He only brings out the cross when girls are around.
I've been in the mood for nachos.
It's the international sign for skateboarding.

He only brings out the cross when girls are around.
He's a genius, it's just no one knows.
It's the international sign for skateboarding.
Yeah, I'm stupid.

He's a genius, it's just no one knows.
Are you kidding me?
Yeah, I'm stupid.
Sometimes you get so fucked up that-

Are you kidding me?
Her mother must have hit her with a pretty stick.
Sometimes you get so fucked up that
all you can say is *I'm so fucked up.*

Her mother must have hit her with a pretty stick.
This mall sucks.
All you can say is *I'm so fucked up.*
Lesson Learned.

This mall sucks.
Ah, shit, man, are you kidding me?
Lesson Learned:
Skater Guys Dig Taco Bell

To the Boy Who Builds and Paints Sets at the Arden Theatre Company in Philadelphia

Oh Boy Who Builds and Paints Sets
at the Arden Theatre Company in Philadelphia!
It is to you that I raise my sneakers,
the ones that you stained when you accidentally
spilled paint on them: Parillo Red 158
the color of my cheeks after you kept apologizing
and apologizing and apologizing.

Oh Boy Who Builds and Paints Sets
at the Arden Theatre Company in Philadelphia!
It is to you that I raise my humus and tofu sandwich,
the one that I've bought everyday since you told me
about the restaurant, hands on hips, tool belt slouching,
extolling the virtues of protein in a vegetarian's diet.

Oh Boy Who Builds and Paints Sets
at the Arden Theatre Company in Philadelphia!
It is to you that I raise my eyes, my eyebrows,
my expectations but not my head as I walk swiftly
and suspiciously past the stage again hoping that you
will call out my name so that I can answer back:
Yes, Perry!

Who was your mother, Perry, so that I can thank her.
Did she have paint-stained hands as well? Will your
children? Will the neo-natal nurses get red-faced,
scrubbing your infant's tiny flecked fingers
with lava soap and a bristle brush?

Will you build your children dramatic cradles
and paint them with non-toxic inks?

I fantasize about you working constantly
and not just building sets, but your old jobs
as well, using information that I gleaned
from the only true conversation we've ever had,
that time in the green room backstage when you
ate M&M's and drank Yoo-Hoo.

The images of a past you roll around in my head:

The you that worked at the Healthfood store!
The you that worked at the Florist!
The you that worked as a Chocolate Inspector
at a factory in Hershey!

You said that they fired you
because you ate too much candy.
Are you stealing from here as well?
Are you building sets in
your backyard, and praying for actors to come?

If I had the money I would buy you
all the loose and loopy corduroys
that your armoires could hold. I would raid
Salvation Armies for those grade school tee-shirts
that hug your long and narrow columns of tight ribs
and flesh. I would buy you even more of those glasses
that are too big for your face, so that you can look sloppy
and curious pushing the frames up with the one finger
you keep paint free.

I would flood your bathroom with Lava soap.

But alas, oh Boy Who Builds and Paints
Sets at the Arden Theatre Company in Philadelphia!

Oh Boy Who the Gods and the Angels and the Interns
and the Actors and your Mother call Perry! You do not
care for the playwright upstairs nor for the secretaries
who click their tongues at the paint you spill in the
stairwell. Or for the silly actresses who giggle
and gossip that you're gay.

Nor do you care for this stuttering girl
with her paint-stained shoes who shyly watches you
from the mezzanine, pressing herself up against the wall,
feeling her own small heat.

You only care about the set and the paint
and the play which has not even been cast yet
but for which you have already built the world.

LORI

How could you
like 3 girls with this
lame-ass name and
not like me?

I have a good vocabulary
and more than adequate
handwriting.

RYAN

Of all the names that can be given
to a boy at his birth it was this name
that the gods destined I would develop
the most crushes on. I guess they figured
because I was a poet and you know:
Ryan
Crying

Roadtrip, Front Seat, Tennessee, 2:37am

I suck on an orange fruit ball.

This is what
your mouth tastes like
on long car trips

because coffee makes you
jumpy and you don't like soda.

America is the most beautiful
when seen from the highway
at 3am.

There is a gentleness
shared among the drivers
at night. There is no ego
on a highway at 3am.

Only concepts of destination
and soft orange fruit balls.

I want to kiss you,
but instead I push another
candy past my lips.

Outside, the highway
stretches in front of us
like the opposite of a metaphor,
like the flipside of our flesh,
like extensions of our dull nerves,
like a dry tongue.

EUROPE

It's odd the way
we associate places
with people.

When I went to Paris,
I collected pebbles
every time I thought
of you.

I meant to present them
to you upon my return.

For once my love
was going to be something
tangible: A big rattling
bottle of thought.

But I lost my intention,
and scattered the pebbles
with the stones on your driveway.

Now I feel stupid, treading
against their meaning as I find
my way to your porch
for yet another
platonic breakfast.

BAR HARBOR

We rode into a sleeping Maine harbor town
thirteen days before he would leave
for upstate New York and a job in publishing.

We'd been driving for hours, the moonlight
casting shadows through our windows,
thunder against our twilight skins

and caught the second-to-last ferry.
Soon we were buried in the silent milk mist
of a cool July after-night. He told me

I reminded him of something from his childhood,
something sweet and thick like bakery air.
I smiled and the air was so crisp it broke

like waves on our faces. He looked old,
filling an old french fry box
with cigarette butts. The night was tugging

at our mouths, but we remained silent.
I wanted to press his eyes on the smooth
spaces of my reasons but I was caught

somewhere between his hands and
Philadelphia. I kept all the words
I should have said, and in my dreams

I rip those words out of my sewn mouth,
all those the tiny pieces of would-have-been us.
But in real life, we found our way

to the opposite shore,
the silence collecting in our veins.
But not before I took his hand and together

we watched the moon peel off
another of clouds, proving to us again
that it is nothing, but distance and reflection.

August in Philadelphia

It is the night before I leave for New York City
and the leaves spin their last dance for me
the branches, crooked and indifferent,
shut the moon out as it rises over
a staccato silhouette of buildings

There's a song for Philadelphia
written in ripened sidewalk bruises
vibrating along the soles
of worn down boots, a chorus of
dandelions, pretzel vendors, blue-black pigeons,
it creaks in our histories, our voices

it's a decadent song, playing with black girls
that skip rope on East Ontario
they sing through smiling gap teeth
they pull up their tiny jointed limbs
dancing over beating rhythm,
rope on concrete, I've danced this dance too.

The songs run through our blood, our streets,
I can follow you the sounds through water
in rain and faucets, opened hydrants,
pipes ringing in Gramma's house,
the sprinklers in the front yard to cool
the round-bellied toddlers

My last night, and I'm lying in bed.
Down the street I hear an old woman singing,
her voice scratching a skyline
which looks like a garden of jewels.

This Place, 1996

There was a church and
I've never seen this church
I've never prayed there,

but I read an article
about it at work
just another burning,

as if it's become normal,
as if things become less sacred.

I pray in the bathroom
when no one else is there.

I work on the eleventh floor
and it gets so quiet sometimes.
I run my fingers over the planes
of my face, and thank god for
mouths, thank god for hands
and eyes and hair, thank god
for arms.

I have never been down south.
Florida doesn't count, and
neither does driving through it.

I never looked at their faces
so I can't tell you anything.

there was this church
far from where I pull

my shadows now.
I'm on the eleventh floor
in the city, where being
barefoot doesn't get me
any closer to the ground.

Yesterday

If it was a game,
you won.

If you wanted me to surrender,
hand me the white flag.

Uncle. Uncle. Uncle.

DOWN THERE

This is how you refer to your genitals.
This is also where your mother told me,
while standing at the basement door,
I could find some ice cream.

I Love You

the last time you
said this to me
we were still
in high school.

I never said it
to you.

and although
I wish
it were different

we will probably
never say it
to each other again.

which is why
you will never
read this book.

Too Many: Twice

This is the ratio of the number of poems
I've written about you to the number of times
you've called me back.

CHROME GRAVITY

Ben and I woke up before the sun
every Saturday morning in September
making sure we were brushed and presentable
by eight at the latest and met on his porch
before the day could even say the word love

By October, we were meeting at six
he'd be sleepy-eyed and grinning, still unfocused
and crooked on the couch when I knocked
his parents would be asleep so we would creep
around the house trying to find his shoes and a hat
before we hit the gravel and walked a half a mile
to Suburban House Diner, the best in the world
and only three city blocks in from Bucks County

We found our table in mid-November
it was made of plastic and glitter,
didn't have one cigarette burn,
was close to the jukebox and the bathroom
and the only booth in the whole joint
that had a number: thirty-eight
we christened it with coffee spills

We'd watch traffic and people
and ordered a different omelet every week
in December, we even saw Santa eating
chipped beef on Christmas Eve, complaining
about business and giving all the waitress
candy canes and reindeer made of pipe cleaners.

Ben and I found romance swimming in pineapple juice
one bleary eyed January morning when the frost
had just begun to creep into the sidewalk cracks
and we were just kids from the other side of County Line
holding hands under the table, rushing our meals
to get back home.

In February, they took the jukebox out for repairs
and said they weren't sure if it was coming back
it was expensive to fix and didn't really
bring in a lot of money
we frowned
over our pancakes and over-priced waffles
Valentine's Day was silent and white,
snow falling like ribbon, spreading
thin its welcome, the truck drivers cursing.

Ben called last night,
and it was the first time I heard his voice
since March when we finished our breakfasts in silence
and walked home in different directions
stiffing the waitress and adding a new chill
to the crisp spring air

He spoke about the magic of the diner
and how they just redid the interior
for Easter. They even added a new omelet
some sacrilege creation in the form of a cross
and they installed a new jukebox,
he said, it plays all the old stuff,
it plays all the old stuff like memories.

KATIE

This is the girl who broke my brother's heart.
I told him that if I ever saw her again
I would kick the crap out of her.
This seemed to cheer him up significantly,
even though we both knew
I wouldn't actually do it.
However, nothing says that
the person reading this can't beat her up.
Come on. I want my brother to be happy,
don't you?

MARC

In the 7th grade,
you said that you wouldn't date me
because I wasn't your type.

The next time I saw you, you were
working full time at the Super Fresh,
bagging groceries and keeping
the parking lot in order.

After I was done shopping,
I pushed my shopping cart
halfway down the road and left it
half-submerged in a swampy puddle.

Hell hath no fury
like a 12-year-old scorned.

Lit

(or for the Scientist to Whom I'm Not Speaking Anymore)

Don't say you didn't see this coming, Jason.

Don't say you didn't realize this would be my reaction
and that you never intended for me to get all worked up,
because if that were true, then you are dumber
than Lenny from Mice and Men, blinder than Oedipus
and Tiresias put together and can feel less
than a Daulton Trumbo character.

You put the Dick in Dickens and the Boo in kowski
and are more Coward-ly then Noël.

But you don't understand any of these references,
Do you, Jason? Because you "don't read."
You are a geology major and you once told me
that "scientists don't read popular literature,
Cristin, we have more important things to do."

Well, fuck you.

Be glad you don't read, Jason,
because maybe you won't understand this
as I scream it to you on your front lawn,
on Christmas Day, brandishing
three hypodermic needles, a ginsu knife
and a letter of permission
from Bret Easton Ellis.

Jason, you are more absurd than Ionesco.
You are more abstract than Joyce,

more inconsistent than Agatha Christie
and more Satanic than Rushdie's verses.

I can't believe I used to want to Sappho you, Jason.
I used to want to Pablo Neruda you,
to Anaïs Nin And Henry Miller you. I used to want
to be O for you, to blow for you in ways
that even Odysseus' sails couldn't handle.
But self-imposed illiteracy isn't a turn-on.

You used to make fun of me being a writer,
saying "Scientists cure diseases,
what do writers do?"

But of course, you wouldn't understand, Jason.
I mean, have you ever gotten an inner thirsting
for Zora Neale Hurston?
Or heard angels herald for you
to read F. Scott Fitzgerald?
Have you ever had a beat attack for Jack Kerouac?
The only Morrison you know is Jim, and you think
you're the noble one?

Go Plath yourself.

Your heart is so dark, that even Joseph Conrad
couldn't see it, and it is so buried under bullshit
that even Poe's cops couldn't hear it.

Your mind is as empty as the libraries in Fahrenheit 451.
Your mind is as empty as Silas Marner's coffers.
Your mind is as empty as Huckleberry Finn's wallet.
And some people might say that this poem
is just a pretentious exercise

in seeing how many literary references
I can come up with.

And some people might complain that this poem is,
at its core, shallow, expressing the same emotion again,
and again, and again. I mean, how many times
can you articulate your contempt for Jason,
before the audience gets a little bored.

But you know what, Jason? Those people
would be wrong. Because this is not the poem
I am writing to express my hatred for you.

This poem is the poem I am writing because
we aren't speaking, and it is making my heart hurt
so bad, that sometimes I can't make it up of the floor.

And this is the poem I am writing instead of writing
the *I miss having breakfast with you* poem, instead
of the *Let's walk dogs in our old schoolyard
again* poem. Instead of the *How are you doing?* poem,
the *I miss you* poem, the *I wish I was making fun
of how much you like Garth Brooks while sitting
in front of your parents' house in your jeep* poem,
instead of the *Holidays are coming around and
you know what that means: SUICIDE!* poem.

I am writing this so that I can stop wanting to write
the *I could fall in love with you again so quickly
if only you would say one more word to me* poem.

But I am tired of loving you, Jason
'cause you don't love me right.

And if some pretentious ass poem can stop me
From thinking about the way your laugh sounds,
about the way your skin feels in the rain,
about how I would rather be miserable with you,
than happy with anyone else in the world,

If some pretentious ass poem can do all that?

Then I am gone with the wind, I am on the road,
I have flown over the fucking cuckoo's nest,
I am gone, I am gone, I am gone.

I am.

YES

I woke up this morning
and thought of you while
I was brushing my teeth.

I smiled.

That's the poem right there.

ACKNOWLEDGMENTS

Grateful acknowledgements are made to the following publications or CDs in which some of these writings first appeared in slightly different forms:
Poetry Slam: The Competitive of Art of Performance Poetry, Will Work for Peace: New Political Poems, Manifold, Mirror, The Waverly Review, Voiceworks: The Australian Youth Quarterly, My Love in a Petri Dish, nycSLAMS, Word Warriors: 25 WomenLeaders in the Spoken Word Revoluiton.

ABOUT THE AUTHOR

CRISTIN O'KEEFE APTOWICZ is the author of *Dear Future Boyfriend, Hot Teen Slut, Working Class Represent* and *Oh, Terrible Youth* (all published by The Wordsmith Press). Founder of the three-time National Poetry Slam Championship venue, NYC-Urbana, Aptowicz has performed her work on such diverse stages as Australia's Sydney Opera House, Joe's Pub in NYC and the Paramount Theatre in Seattle, as well as at universities and festivals around the world. She lives in New York City and when not on tour, she usually can be found at the Bowery Poetry Club.

For more information on the author (including schedules of upcoming performances), please visit her website: http://www.aptowicz.com

For more information on The Wordsmith Press, please visit our website: